PICTURE THE WORLD OF
FLYING MACHINES

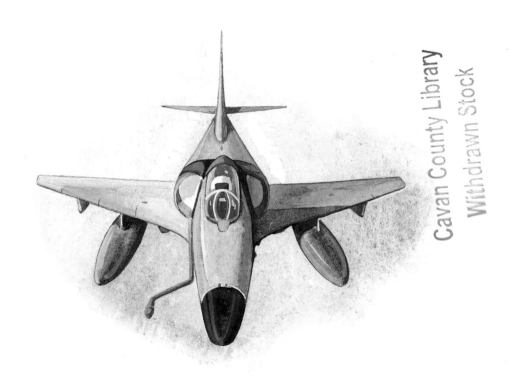

AWARD PUBLICATIONS LIMITED

Faster than sound

Concorde is the only airliner that travels so fast that it goes more than twice the speed of sound. By the time we hear it, it has already gone past us! Concorde can fly across the Atlantic Ocean between Britain and America in just three-and-a-half hours. Compared with other passenger airliners, Concorde is smaller and has two unique features; its delta wings, and its nose which tilts down for landing and take-off, or when travelling at slower speeds. It is 62 metres long and has a wing-span of 26 metres. It can carry 136 passengers.

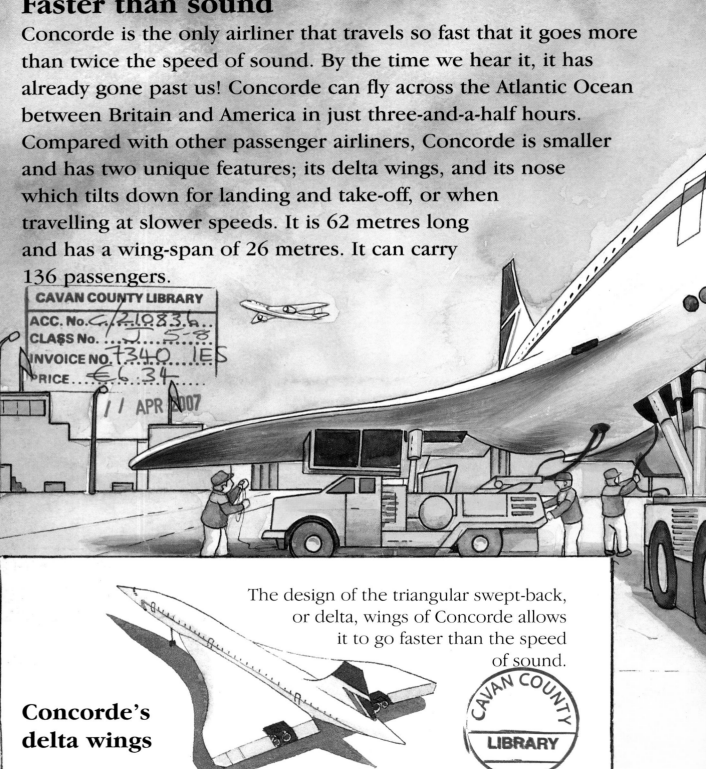

The design of the triangular swept-back, or delta, wings of Concorde allows it to go faster than the speed of sound.

Concorde's delta wings

Lighter than air

An airship is a power-driven balloon. Modern airships have an envelope, like a balloon, made of flexible fabric, which is mostly filled with helium. Helium is a gas which is lighter than air, so it lifts the airship. Engines fixed to the gondola or cabin underneath the balloon drive propellers which can be swivelled to move the airship in different directions. Airships move quite slowly and can hover easily, making them useful for filming events such as football matches.

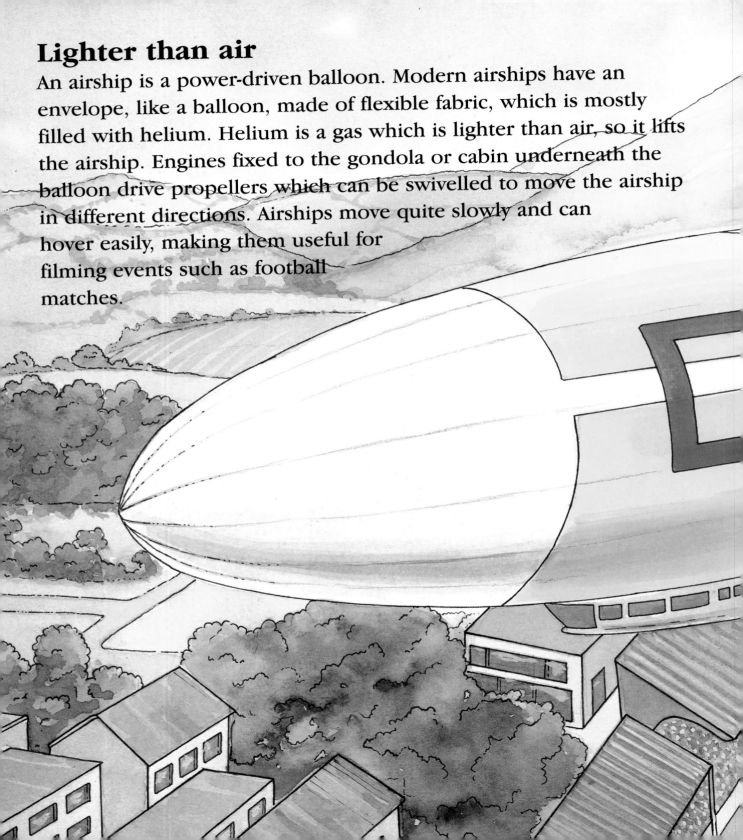

Flying to faraway places

Because we can travel very quickly from one continent to another the world now seems a much smaller place. There are many types of passenger aircraft and this Boeing 747, or Jumbo Jet, can carry over 500 passengers. It has two decks and can fly over 13,000 kilometres without having to refuel.

Landing on water

Aircraft that can land on water are called seaplanes. They are used in places where it would be difficult to make a landing strip for normal aircraft. In jungles or forests, seaplanes can set down on a river or a lake, and they are also ideal for flying between islands. Instead of wheels, seaplanes have light, hollow floats beneath their wings.

Fighters

Fighters are special planes which are built to travel very fast. They are usually small and often carry only the pilot. In combat they are armed with guns, missiles and sometimes bombs.

This Harrier Jump Jet, at an airshow, is showing how it can take off and land vertically, like a helicopter. This means it can fly from a small area, such as a forest clearing, where it can be easily hidden from enemy bombers. It can also take off and land like a normal fighter but needs only a short runway.

Silent flight

A glider plane has no engine. It relies on warm air currents, called thermals, to keep it airborne. It has to be towed up into the air by a small powered aircraft, a truck or a winch. A hang glider is a small rigid wing with a harness below for the pilot to lie in. It is made of fabric supported by a strong, light frame. A paraglider is a gliding parachute. Both can be launched from a hilltop.

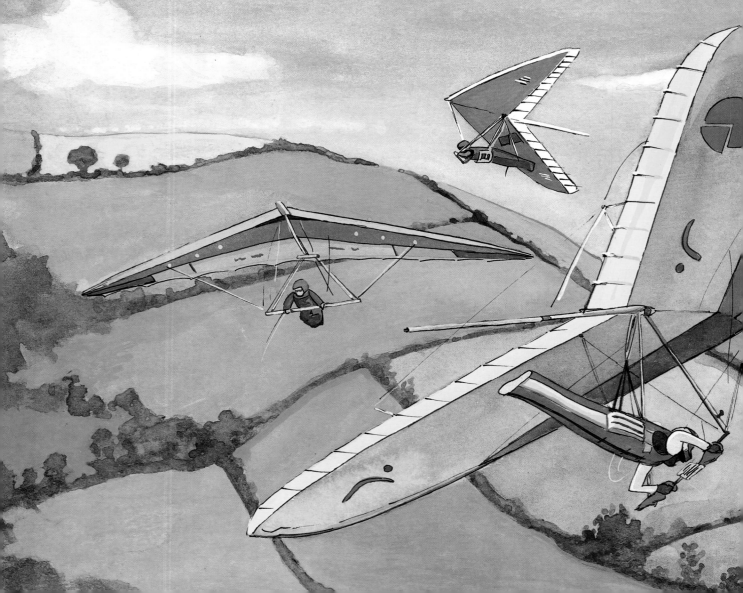

Look, no wings!

Helicopters are aircraft without wings; instead, they have spinning blades called rotors. Most helicopters have a main rotor near the front that lifts the helicopter up, and a small one at the back for steering. They can land or take off from any small flat area by

going straight up or down. In an emergency situation, a helicopter can lift an injured person and get them to hospital much more quickly than an ambulance can by road.

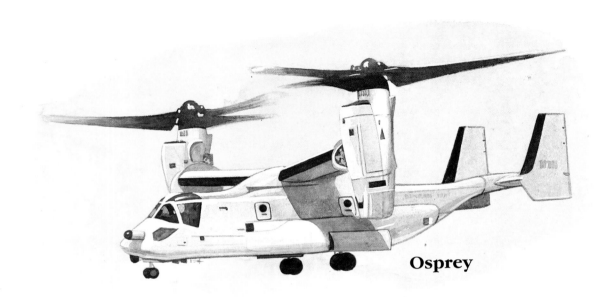

Osprey

ISBN 0-86163-967-7

Copyright © 1999 Award Publications Limited

First published 1999
Second impression 2002

Published by Award Publications Limited,
27 Longford Street, London NW1 3DZ

Printed in Singapore